This Book Belongs To:

....

I am..................years old.

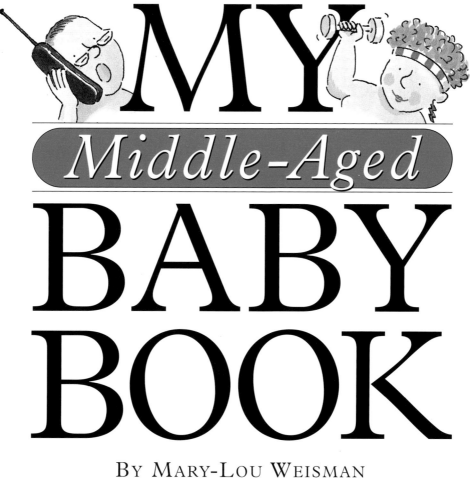

MY *Middle-Aged* BABY BOOK

By Mary-Lou Weisman

ILLUSTRATED BY PAUL MEISEL

Workman Publishing • New York

LIBRARY OF CONGRESS CATALOGING-IN-PUBLICATION DATA
WEISMAN, MARY-LOU
MY MIDDLE-AGED BABY BOOK BY MARY-LOU WEISMAN
P. CM.
ISBN 1-56305-817-0
1. MIDDLE AGE—HUMOR. I. TITLE.
PN6162.W448 1995
818'.5402—DC20   95-19449
CIP

ILLUSTRATIONS COPYRIGHT ©1995 BY PAUL MEISEL

WORKMAN BOOKS ARE AVAILABLE AT A SPECIAL DISCOUNT WHEN PURCHASED IN
BULK FOR SPECIAL PREMIUMS AND SALES PROMOTIONS AS WELL AS FOR FUND-
RAISING OR EDUCATIONAL USE. SPECIAL EDITIONS OR BOOK EXCERPTS CAN ALSO
BE CREATED TO SPECIFICATION. FOR DETAILS, CONTACT THE SPECIAL SALES
DIRECTOR AT THE ADDRESS BELOW.

WORKMAN PUBLISHING COMPANY, INC.
708 BROADWAY
NEW YORK, NY 10003

MANUFACTURED IN THE UNITED STATES OF AMERICA

FIRST PRINTING SEPTEMBER 1995
10 9 8

Acknowledgments

I'd like to take this opportunity to acknowledge all the middle-aged amnesiacs who have contributed to making this book an overnight best-seller. First I want to thank my editor, Ruth... Ruth...Darn! It's right on the tip of my tongue!...Oh, and I especially appreciate the expertise of gastroenterologist Dr. Harvey... Ummm Harvey... And, of course, the host of friends too unforgettable to mention, not the least of whom is my patient, supportive husband...what's his name?...

CONTENTS

My Vital Statistics

(PHOTO HERE)

Here I Am

I'm a girl.......... boy.......... *(check one)*

Name: ....
.......(FIRST)....................(MIDDLE)....................(FAMILY NAME)

Married name(s): ....

I am .... years old/not telling ....

Weight: .... Length: ....

Circumference of head: ....

Circumference of abdomen: ....

Inseam/Bra size:...

Social Security number: ....

Driver's license: ....

Home phone: ....

Business phone: ....

Car phone: ....

Fax: ....

Answering machine remote code: ....

E-mail: ....

PIN: ....

Donor card: ....

Credit cards: Visa .... Mastercard .... American Express ....

    EXPIRATION DATES: ....

Cholesterol count (and HDLs): ....

Blood pressure: ....

Locker combination: ....
                        (RIGHT)   (LEFT)   (RIGHT)

Other: ....

MAKE YOUR OWN FAMILY TREE

Sperm Donor

Person I most look like

Marriage held together by Zoloft

Just signed up for tap lessons

Still smokes in the bathroom

Always does Thanksgiving

Made money in junk bonds

Won't go in a home

Married a woman half his age

Suspected dyslexic

Never writes thank you notes

Has my brains (and thighs)

Good with his stepchildren

Cute, but spoiled

Offered early retirement

Biological clock running out

Memorable Firsts

My first tooth lost:...

My first colonoscopy: ....

My first reading glasses:..

My first gray hair:...

My first gray pubic hair:..

My first second mortgage:...

My first isolated hiccup:...

My first conservative opinion: ....

My first involuntary release of urine while sneezing:.............................

My first:...

My first:...

My first:...

My Bottle

Formula	*Response*
❑ DEWARS (6 oz.) ....Very sleepy	
Rocks, splash water	
❑ MARGARITA (10 oz.) ....Very sleepy	
Cuervo Gold tequila, fresh	
lime, salt, straight up	
❑ MOLSON (6-pack)..Very sleepy	
Golden, chilled	
❑ CHARDONNAY (16 oz.) ....Very sleepy	
Louis La Tour, chilled	
❑ MERLOT (16 oz.) ....Awful headache	
Santa Rita, room temp	
❑	
(MINE)	

AM I A GIRL OR A BOY?

That depends. Do you spend most of your time in front of the toilet, running water, or naked on the lawn, rolling in snow?

Usually at about the age of 50, both men and women go through profound physical changes: women are no longer able to bear children and men are no longer able to pee. This is not bad. This is natural.

As is too often the case with matters involving sexuality, ignorance and fear are the worst enemies.

Just a very few years ago, women wouldn't even talk among themselves behind closed doors about menopause. No one wanted to be associated with the stereotypical sexless, moody hag in a house dress who went about flinging open windows, hurling epithets and sprouting chin hairs. But as soon as the first change-of-life revolutionary stepped out of the closet wearing a white silk blouse, hoop earrings, three-inch heels and a face-lift, and spoke the words, "Is it hot in here or is it me?" the dread taboo was broken. Menopause began to catch on. The hot flash gained instant cachet. Watching one come and go became an event to rival a childbirth video or the aurora borealis.

Soon menopause was selling more tabloids than an Elvis sighting. Women began drying their sweaty linens in public. They discussed the side effects of Provera on *Nightline*. Vaginal dryness was on *Oprah*. The public, once in love with celebrities who had been abused as children, now turned their fickle attention to celebrities going through menopause in public. It is only a matter of time before Shirley MacLaine will write a book about her prior-life menopause as an Egyptian princess. Madonna will star in a made-for-menopause video, "Can't Wait to Get Hot All Over." Mary Beth Whitehead will be looking for a menopause surrogate to have hers. Michael Jackson will volunteer. Inevitably, Elizabeth Taylor will be rushed to Cedars Sinai Medical Center, comatose from an accidental overdose of estrogen. After six months or so, figure on some backlash in the form of a new 12-step, self-help program—menstrual daughters of menopausal mothers.

If media exposure can

make a celebrity out of menopause, imagine what a little public awareness might do for involuntary urine retention. The prostate is the most misunderstood, mispronounced gland in the male body. (The people who call it the "prostrate" are the same people who call nuclear, "nucular.") When asked, "Where is it?" nine out of ten men answer, "Down there." The tenth will venture a guess. "It's what the doctor is looking for when he holds your balls and asks you to cough." How big is it? "Uh. . . dunno. It's either the size of a marble, or a golf ball or a baseball." (Men like to think of their inner body parts as sporting goods. Women imagine produce.)

What does the prostate do? Nobody's sure. Either it makes sperm, stores sperm or ejaculates sperm. What is prostate trouble? It's when you want to pee but you can't pee. (Why are men so ignorant about their bodies in general and their penises in particular? First they go to all the trouble of giving them names, and then they don't even want to get to know them!) Only excruciating pain and the fear of exploding get their attention. Then they want to know. Then they'll see a doctor. Only then, when the doctor inserts his index finger in their rectums to palpate the swollen gland, do they learn where the prostate is. Only then do they find out that the gland, which has enlarged to the size of a hockey puck, is obstructing the flow of urine from their bladder, which is now the size of a basketball.

Only when they are under local anesthesia and see the surgeon coming straight at them brandishing a 6-foot periscope mounted with a bayonet will they develop a healthy respect for the prostate. Its swelling will be celebrated as a middle-aged rite of passage. There will be chants and drumbeats. This could be a hard sell. Call in Clint Eastwood.

First Recognizes Self

Teething

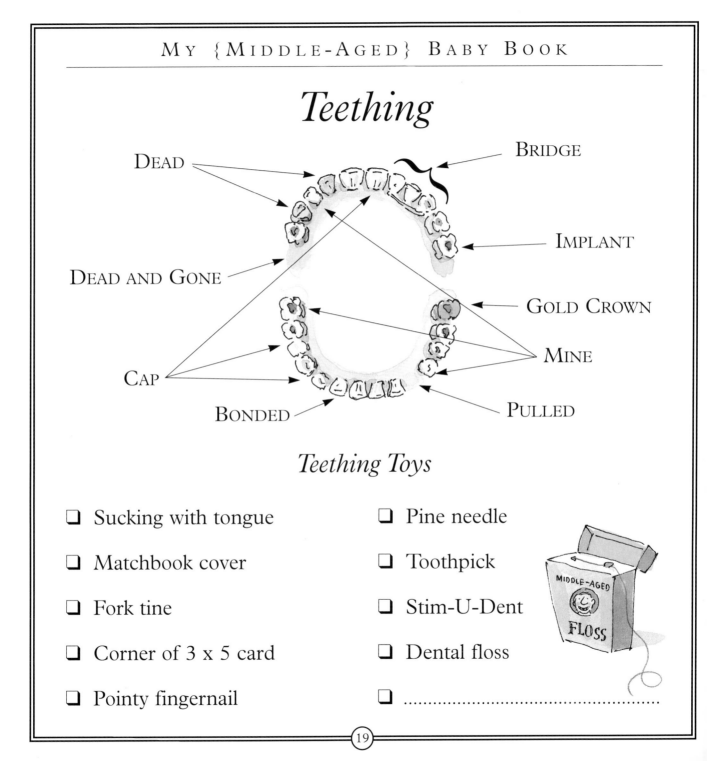

DEAD

BRIDGE

DEAD AND GONE

IMPLANT

GOLD CROWN

MINE

CAP

BONDED

PULLED

Teething Toys

- ❏ Sucking with tongue
- ❏ Matchbook cover
- ❏ Fork tine
- ❏ Corner of 3 x 5 card
- ❏ Pointy fingernail

- ❏ Pine needle
- ❏ Toothpick
- ❏ Stim-U-Dent
- ❏ Dental floss
- ❏ ....

INTRODUCING SOLID FOODS

10,459 B.C. • The Evolutionary Diet. Early person's diet consists mostly of take-out—nuts, berries, roots, and tubers. They make fire, but fail to invent french fries. They shoot buffalo, but don't eat wings. There is no dessert. They consume only organically grown food but don't know it's health food. Early people don't even know they're on the Pritikin diet, although they do notice that they're passing a lot of gas.

Alternate Creationist Diet. All the fruit you can eat, except apples.

The Savage Special. The eating of red meat has a special allure for early persons not concerned with political or ecological correctness. Tribal people ascribe magical homeopathic qualities to eating free-range meat. Eating tiger makes a person brave and strong. Rabbit makes one timid. People who suffer from lethargy eat ants. Owl's eyes, like carrots, help a person to see in the dark. If you want to have the strength of your enemy, the best way to get it is to eat him. "You are what you eat" is taken literally.

7,000 B.C. • The Rise of Bread. The innocent age of hunting and gathering is brought to an abrupt end by the development of agriculture in the Neolithic Period, specifically the cultivation of grain, and the subsequent discovery of beer, corn chips, and the resting pulse. The appearance of the first fat person.

250 A.D. • The Romans Invent Bulimia.

1894 • The First Hershey Bar.

1900 – 1930 • The Age of Analysis. The seven basic food groups are taught in the public schools, but people can only remember "green and leafy vegetables." The discovery of the calorie reveals a causal link between eating too much and weighing too much. Fat people are seen lacking in self-control. Their claims of malfunctioning thyroids and slow metabolisms are dismissed as bogus and self-serving.

More people get fat.

1931 • THE DAWN OF DIETING.
The first diets were predicated on
the theory of rapid transit: the
faster the food moves through
the body, the smaller the
weight gain. The Grapefruit-
and-an-Enema Diet and The
Banana-and-an-Enema Diet
attract few adherents. Jell-O,
the first real diet food,
inspires the first enema-free
diet dish: cottage cheese,
Jell-O cubes, canned peach
halves in heavy syrup, and a
maraschino cherry. The
Duchess of Windsor is the first
to link wealth and thinness. Even
more people get fat.

1949 • THE CLEAN PLATE CLUB
OF AMERICA. Membership reaches
an all-time high.

**1950 – 1960 • THE DARK
AGES OF DIETING.** Pizza is
named the eighth food group.
Bacon is thought to contain
important minerals. Sara Lee
says, "Let them eat cake."
More and more people get
fatter and fatter. People
weigh themselves only errati-
cally, and often with their
shoes on.

1963 • THE FIRST TAB.

**1981 – 1990 • THE
ENLITENMENT.** Cholesterol is dis-
covered and counted. Polys are
unsaturated. Stouffer says, "Let
there be lite," and there is lite and

extra lite, and lo cal and no cal. Socialite "Babe" Paley says, "You can't be too rich or too thin." Headmistress Jean Harris shoots Diet Doctor Herman Tarnower. People weigh themselves daily and continue to gain weight.

1993 • OPRAH LOSES 60 POUNDS.

1993 • PAVAROTTI GAINS IT.

1994 • THE GREAT DEPRESSION.

Government studies show that dieting rarely results in permanent weight loss (the Yo-Yo Ma factor). Liposuction and the dawn of Invasive Dieting.

2,000 — THE MILLENNIUM OF PERMANENT WEIGHT LOSS.

Surgery replaces willpower. The primitive practice of liposuction is abandoned in favor of organectomy, the removal of one or more specified, nonessential internal body organs or a radical dietectomy, the removal of all nonessential and redundant organs. Gall bladder (1 ounce); spleen (10 ounces); a kidney (5 ounces); a lung (16 ounces); tonsils (1 ounce); appendix (1/2 ounce). Total permanent weight loss: 2 pounds, 1½ ounces.

I Grow Hair

Color: .... Real color: ....

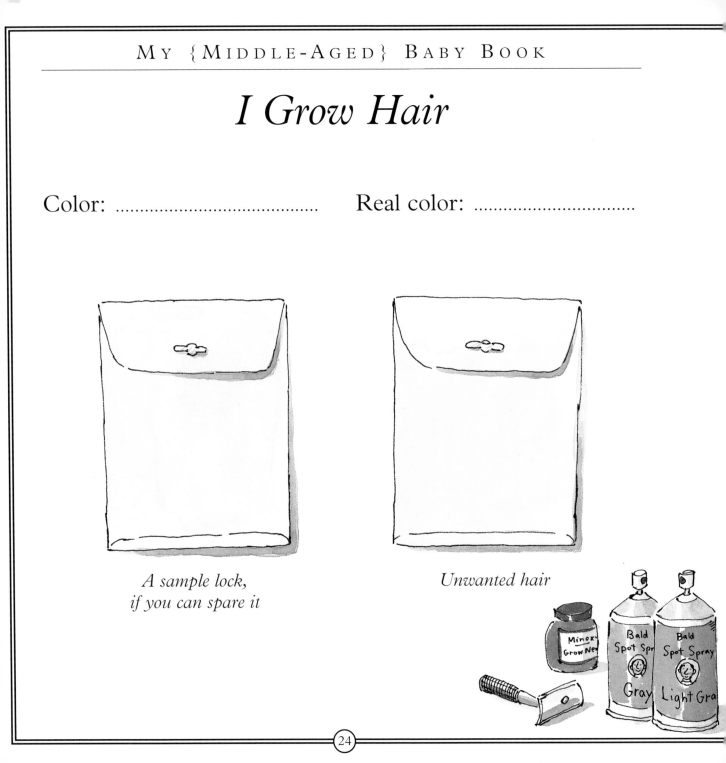

*A sample lock,
if you can spare it*

Unwanted hair

The Seven Stages of Men's Hair Loss

- ❑ Tries minoxidil
- ❑ Parts hair closer to ear
- ❑ Arranges hair strands in snail-like pattern on anterior of head
- ❑ Tries hair plugs
- ❑ Joins hair club
- ❑ Grows beard
- ❑ Shaves head

The Seven Stages of Women's Hair Coloring

- ❑ Pulls out gray hairs
- ❑ Tries henna rinse
- ❑ Has hair highlighted
- ❑ Dyes hair original color
- ❑ Decides to let it go gray
- ❑ Streaks the gray with blond
- ❑ Dyes it champagne blond

I Dress Myself

Fashion Firsts for Big Boys

Switches from jockies to boxers ....

(FILL IN DATE)

Develops appreciation for hats ....

Stops wearing knit shirts ....

Considers suspenders ....

Tosses Speedo ....

Is drawn to vertical stripes ....

Buys first jeans with low rise ....

Wears shirts out ....

Buys Italian designer suit ....

Wears sweats everywhere but work ....

....

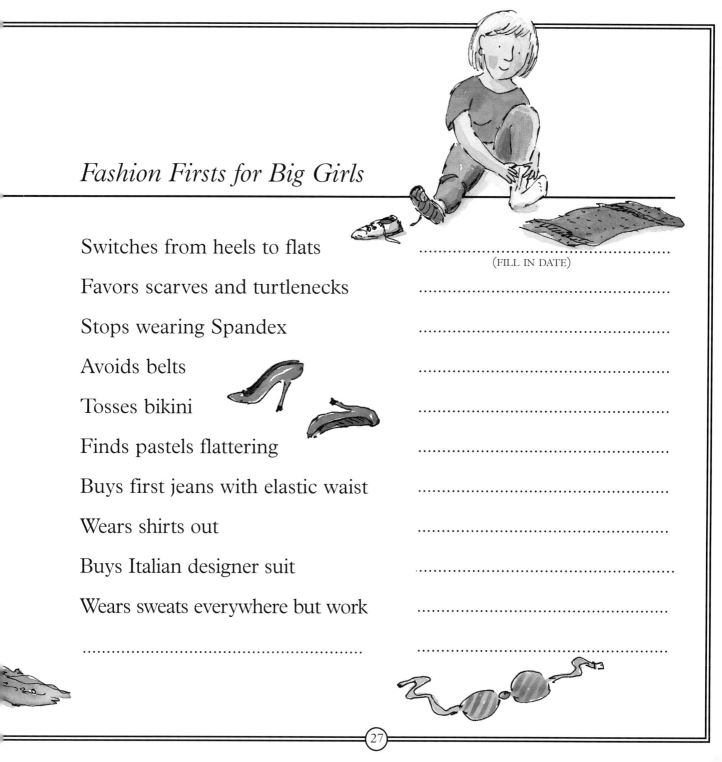

Fashion Firsts for Big Girls

Switches from heels to flats ....
(FILL IN DATE)

Favors scarves and turtlenecks ....

Stops wearing Spandex ....

Avoids belts ....

Tosses bikini ....

Finds pastels flattering ....

Buys first jeans with elastic waist ....

Wears shirts out ....

Buys Italian designer suit ....

Wears sweats everywhere but work ....

....

My Primary Care Givers

HAIRDRESSER:...TEL:.................

INTERNIST:...TEL:..................

PODIATRIST:..TEL:.................

UROLOGIST:...TEL:...................

NUTRITIONIST:..TEL:..................

NEUROLOGIST:...TEL:...................

PSYCHOLOGIST:...TEL:...................

PROCTOLOGIST:...TEL:..................

GYNECOLOGIST:..TEL:...................

DERMATOLOGIST:..TEL:..................

RADIOLOGIST:..TEL:..................

REFLEXOLOGIST:...TEL:..................

OPHTHALMOLOGIST: ....TEL: ....

RHEUMATOLOGIST: ....TEL: ....

ENDOCRINOLOGIST: ....TEL: ....

ELECTROLOGIST: ....TEL: ....

OTOLARYNGOLOGIST: ....TEL: ....

GASTROENTEROLOGIST: ....TEL: ....

PSYCHOPHARMACOLOGIST: ....TEL: ....

MANICURIST: ....TEL: ....

FINANCIAL ADVISER: ....TEL: ....

ASTROLOGER: ....TEL: ....

PERSONAL TRAINER: ....TEL: ....

LAWYER: ....TEL: ....

PSYCHIC: ....TEL: ....

MASSEUSE: ....TEL: ....

OTHER: ....

Toilet Training

(Check where appropriate)

Make public announcement? Yes .... No ....

Door open? .... Door closed? ....

Take in cordless phone? Yes .... No ....

Paper Trained? Yes .... No ....

      Newspaper: .... Crossword puzzles: ....

      Magazine: .... Cartoon books: ....

      Catalogues: ....

          Victoria's Secret ....   Seed ....

Look? Yes .... No ....

Engage in self-praise? Yes .... No ....

Make public announcement? Yes .... No ....

My Bedtime Ritual

- ❏ No caffeine after noon
- ❏ No fluids after 8 p.m.
- ❏ Brush and floss
- ❏ Empty bladder
- ❏ Get in bed
- ❏ Set alarm
- ❏ Watch something
- ❏ Empty bladder
- ❏ Have insomnia
- ❏ Watch anything
- ❏ Empty bladder
- ❏ Have insomnia

- ❏ Read something
- ❏ Empty bladder
- ❏ Have insomnia
- ❏ Cry out to a higher being
- ❏ Nuke a pizza

Favorite
Nursery Rhymes

This little piggy has a bunion,
This little piggy's ingrown,
This little piggy's arthritic,
This little piggy's all bone,
And this little piggy cried,
"My feet are killing me,"
All the way home.

Mrs. Dumpty sat on a wall.
Mrs. Dumpty had a great fall.
Osteoporosis and low estrogen
Shattered her hip, so they put in a pin.

Pizza with onions, pizza double cheese,
Pizza with everything but anchovies.
Some like it hot, some like it cold,
Some eat it from the fridge, nine days old.

Old mother Geezer
Went to the freezer
To get her poor self a munch,
But all that was there
Was low-yo to spare
So she went out for Heath Bar Crunch.

VITAMINS 0
CALORIES
2570
per serving
Fiber 0
Fat
695 grams
per serving

One, two
Can't reach my shoe.
Three, four
Can't get off the floor.
Five, six
What a fix.
Seven, eight
Must have put on some weight.
Nine, ten
A big fat hen.

Mary has some dental floss;
She keeps it with her so…
When shish kebab sticks in her teeth,
The lamb is sure to go.

Hickory digital dock
What's happened to the clock?
It blinks time in your eye,
The batteries die,
And it beeps when it should go ticktock.

Jack and Jill
Went through the mill
Of sexual dysfunction;
Jack's fell down,
Jill broke his crown
Without the least compunction.

My Friends

Friends I work with ....

Friends I work out with ....

Friends I've outgrown ....

Friends I'd go on vacation with ....

Friends I went on vacation with ....

Friends installed on autodial ....

Friends on the Season's Greetings list ....

Friends we see as a couple ....

Friends I see alone ....

Friends I keep promising to get together with but never do ....

Friends who are nice, but I don't like them ....

Friends who ....

Likes and Dislikes

LIKE: Catalogue shopping.
DISLIKE: Returning the merchandise.

DISLIKE: College reunions.
LIKE: Looking better than everyone else.

DISLIKE: When airlines overbook.
LIKE: When they pay you to be bumped.

LIKE: 1-800 numbers.
DISLIKE: Being told by a robot that my phone call is important to her, and then put on hold for the next available operator.

LIKE: Telling my dreams.
DISLIKE: Listening to other people's dreams.

DISLIKE: When construction workers whistle.
DISLIKE: When they don't.

LIKE: When the FDA approves a fat substitute.
DISLIKE: When further scientific studies prove the fat substitute causes cancer.

LIKE: When the so-called scientific studies are shown to be faulty.

LIKE:...
DISLIKE:...

My Favorite Expressions

Where did I put my glasses?
I'm a survivor.
Orgasm isn't everything.
Let's eat out.

Has anyone seen my glasses?
I'm an enabler.
Dressing on the side, please.
Just a taste.

I just had them a minute ago.
She's aging badly.
I never thought I'd say that.
What's your fax?

Maybe I left them by the phone.
It's not PC, but . . .
I sound like my mother.
Where's the remote?

Your glasses are on your forehead.
I hardly ever watch TV.
Let's order Chinese.
Life is short.

I CAN READ

Obituary reading begins in middle age and is considered a normal developmental stage. There are those who argue that this new habit represents the maturing person's first concession to the possibility of mortality. They are wrong. A mature person doesn't concede a damn thing. Death is not inevitable. Death is what happens to people who don't take good enough care of themselves. Death is a mistake for which we have only ourselves to blame. Death is what happens when people refuse to profit from the obituaries of others.

Relatively speaking, our parents knew very little about death prevention. And what they knew was often based on ignorance and superstition. They didn't know eggs could kill. They didn't know about the body-mind connection. They couldn't tell brain-dead from really dead. They didn't even have wellness; just health.

As a result they tended to accept the inevitability of their own mortality. Because we are well enough informed about the kinds of life styles, habits, and states of mind that invite death, we can be the first generation to learn to take responsibility for avoiding it.

Learning how to read the obituaries can add years to your life. A quick, cowardly glance at the headlines, just to reassure yourself that everyone who has died is at least a decade or two older than you only brings temporary relief. To keep death permanently at bay, obituaries must be read thoroughly, studied thoughtfully, and deconstructed strictly. The question to keep in mind is not "What did the deceased die of?" but "What did the deceased do wrong that resulted in his or her failure to maintain perpetual wellness?"

Cancer is not a cause of death; smoking is. Heart attacks are not a cause of death; eating fried eggs, hash browns, and bacon every morning is.

Obituary writers, perhaps out of some warped notion of good taste, give us precious little hard information to go on, preferring soothing euphemisms like "natural causes" and "after a long illness" to explicit accusations and I-told-you-so's. Nevertheless, an expert obituary reader can make a blame diagnosis from the kind of evidence that amateurs would be inclined to overlook as boring and irrelevant.

Sometimes you have to read all the way to the apparently innocent tag line to get to the blame behavior. "Mr. So-and-So was a life-long resident of Los Angeles." In this case death was caused by the deceased's stubborn insistence upon living with free radicals in a city where the air quality index is set permanently on "unacceptable."

"Mrs. So-and-So died at her winter home in Boca Raton after a long illness." Melanoma. Not using sun block. Or, if she did use sun block, not using a high enough SPF. There are *explanations* for dying, but no more excuses.

Sometimes an obituary offers multiple choices: "Mr. What's-His-Name, a lawyer with the New York Stock Exchange, was an avid bird-watcher." Can you name the two potential blame behaviors? Mr. What's-His-Name may have died because he did not bother to learn to control his stress levels with bio-feedback and positive imaging. Or, he might have died of Lyme disease because he didn't tuck his trousers into his socks when he went bird-watching, and then neglected to check his body thoroughly for any sign of a circular rash. It hardly matters which one did him in. Deconstructed is deconstructed.

Some obits are a challenge even for the experts. A case in point is the syndicated TV aerobics instructor, dead at the age of 45. He suffered his first and only heart attack while reading an unsensation-al novel in the shade of a recently pruned tree. Even his closest friend, quoted in the obituary, could not identify the blame behavior. "He never smoked. He never drank. He never stopped taking beta carotene.

He was on a fat-free diet. He meditated. He jogged. He took a gram of aspirin every day. He rode a bike. He swam two miles a day. He consulted with his doctor and had a stress test before embarking on any exercise program. He was a frequent flosser. He read *Prevention* magazine. He had achieved his target pulse. He had balanced his polarities. He had a crystal. I don't get it."

He was too self-involved. God doesn't like narcissists.

Sometimes I Pretend...

(Check where appropriate)

❏ I'm a princess/prince.

❏ I could be an anchorperson.

❏ Life is fair.

❏ The speed limit is 80 mph.

❏ I drank eight glasses of water.

❏ I'm going to open a bed
  and breakfast in Vermont.

❏ It's a fat mirror.

❏ Wrinkles give a face character.

❏ I didn't eat that.

❏ ....

❏ ....

First Words

❑ Gotta get up.

❑ Everything hurts.

❑ We should remember to do that more often.

❑ What's the weather like?

❑ My bladder is bursting.

❑ What a night I had!

❑ What a dream I had!

❑ What a day I've got!

❑ I didn't sleep a wink.

❑ Coffee!

❑ ....

Sex?

(Check one)

❏ Yes   ❏ No   ❏ Can't Remember

Middle-aged sex is much more exciting than:

❏ The moist, breathless, throbbing coital passions of youth.

❏ Sneaking into the movies as a senior citizen.

❏ Stairmaster.

❏ ....

I would have sex more often, but . . .

❏ I keep forgetting how much I like it.

❏ The foreplay is too much work.

❏ Nobody asks.

❏ ....

A good time to have sex is:

❑ Spontaneously, right after I've brushed and flossed.

❑ When we're both awake.

❑ After a good cholesterol count.

❑ When the kids have left for college.

❑ ....

Some nice things to say while you're having sex:

❑ Ooooo*ohh!* That's my bad knee.

❑ Is that you or me?

❑ I can't *get* in that position.

❑ Don't roll on the cats!

❑ I'm turning off the TV.

❑ ....

It Hurts

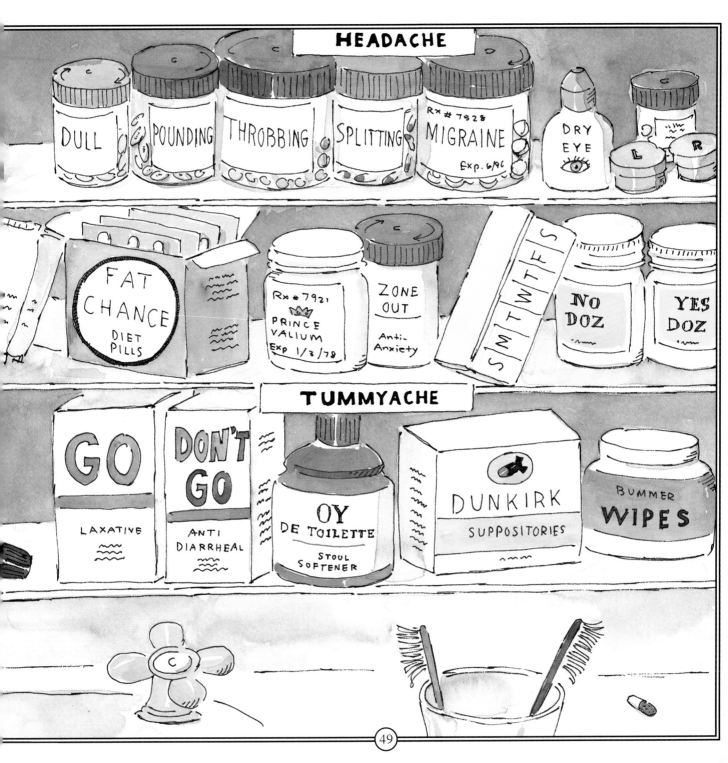

I FORGET

After the age of 30, the brain loses about 100,000 neurons a day. These nerve cells tend to take the car keys with them and leave important things behind, like the words and music to the Mickey Mouse Club theme song. This process is called "forgetting." It does not help to wear a hat.

During a typical 24-hour period, 100,000 neurons can carry off with them the multiplication tables through times 12, the names of all the state capitals, and every joke you've ever heard, including the last one. It is possible to resupply the brain with neurons, and thereby off-set the loss by increasing the flow of high-octane information into the brain. By the time an individual reaches the age of 45, it takes two hours of Swahili instruction, a game of chess with a grand master, and a double-acrostic to make up for a single day of neuron loss. Most people would rather rent a video.

There are two basic kinds of forgetting: losing one's train of thought and losing the passengers on one's train of thought. Losing one's train is caused by a sudden mass defection of neurons. One moment you're moving purposefully toward your destination. The next, you're standing stupidly in the doorway, mentally derailed. *"What did I come in here for?"* Dental floss? A tissue? Nail clippers? You haven't the foggiest. Nothing. Nada. This kind of memory loss brings one to the edge of existential despair, gives one a nauseating glimpse of the abyss, and stuns one with the blunt purpose-lessness of life. *"Why am I here?"* Why, indeed.

Thinking about it doesn't help. Occasionally, through reenactment, one is able to grab hold of the caboose, thereby rescuing one's train in mid-abyss. You retrace your steps, assuming of course that you can remember what it was you were doing immediately before you forgot what it was you came in for. You do. You go to the sink to retrieve the coffee cup and spoon you had been using moments earlier, before the twinkie blackout. You pour a pretend cup of coffee, spoon in a bit of pretend sugar, and pretend-stir it. You pick up the paper and can't see the words. Then you stride purposefully, triumphantly into the next room to get your glasses. You feel grateful that no one is home to witness this embarrassing charade.

At least losing one's train is almost always a private act. Losing the passengers on the train, however, is invariably a public act and therefore potentially more humiliating. Passenger loss is characterized by the annoying yet tantalizing feeling that a word—most often a name—is right on the tip of one's tongue. In fact, it is not. The surname or punch-line bearing neuron has already leapt off the tongue and is airborne.

Just a moment ago, a roomful of people were hanging on your every word. Now they are held hostage while you grope for the lost word as if it were a dropped contact lens. "Wait a second! Hold it! Don't anybody move! I had it just a second ago. He's a famous actor. First name starts with a B. Or an F. You know who I mean. He's a character actor. Plays bad guys. Why can't I think of his name? He's on late night movies all the

time. Westerns, mostly. His name goes like this—Boom. Ba Boom. First name, one syllable; second, two. I think. C'mon. You know this guy. He's always squinting and he walks kinda like this. . . ."

It is considered rude to forget in public. Forgetting, like sneezing, coughing, and burping is an unexpected, unwanted intrusion into the lives of innocent bystanders. Although forgetting is one of the few bodily emissions that does not make its own exit noise, it is invariably accompanied by other behaviors that polite people find at least as offensive. Straining at remembering should be a private act. If forgetting in public does occur, just keep talking. Act as if nothing has happened. It's no big deal. You're just losing your mind. Wave bye-bye.

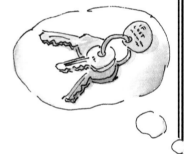

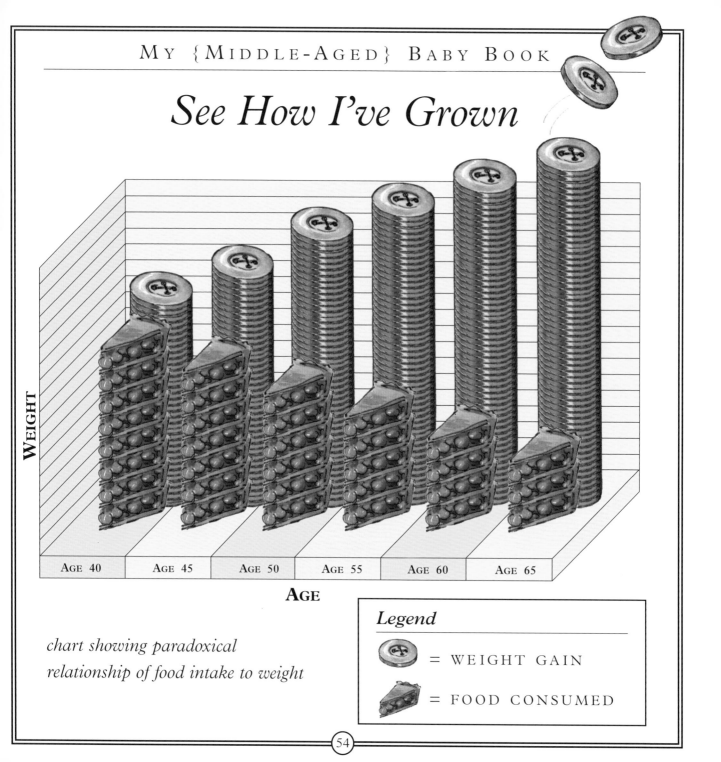

See How I've Grown

Weight

| Age 40 | Age 45 | Age 50 | Age 55 | Age 60 | Age 65 |

Age

chart showing paradoxical relationship of food intake to weight

Legend

= WEIGHT GAIN

= FOOD CONSUMED

See What I've Grown

- ❑ ....
- ❑ Eye flaps
- ❑ Turkey neck
- ❑ Elbow flaps
- ❑ Pot belly
- ❑ Love handles
- ❑ Enlarged prostate
- ❑ ....
- ❑ Corns

- ❑ ....
- ❑ Dewlaps
- ❑ Liver spots
- ❑ Swag arm
- ❑ Pendulous breasts
- ❑ Piles
- ❑ Knee flaps
- ❑ Varicose veins
- ❑ ....

AM I SMILING...

or is it gas?

Q. *Where does intestinal gas come from?*

A. Gastroenterologists divide flatulents into two basic groups: Aerophagics (APs), from the Greek "air swallowers" and Intestinal Producers (IPs), people who manufacture their own internal air. APs tend to be nervous individuals who gulp excessive amounts of air (oxygen, nitrogen, and hydrogen) while talking and eating, drinking, smoking, gum chewing, or sucking breath fresheners.

This swallowed air, along with the air that naturally occurs in staple foods such as diet Cokes and Dairy Queens, lies in the stomach awaiting one of two possible fates: it may be brought up as a burp or expelled as gas. Which way it goes is a function of individual intestinal motility. Flatologists estimate that 50 to 70 percent of all the gas in the digestive tract comes from swallowed air. The remaining 30 to 50 percent is produced in the lower intestine during the fermenting process, called digestion. The resulting gases are expelled rectally. They are the ones that people try to blame on Labrador retrievers or mice decomposing in the walls.

Q. *How can I tell if I'm primarily an Aerophagic or an Intestinal Producer?*

A. An informal, though quite reliable determination can be made nasally: if the odor is aggressively paleolithic, you're an Intestinal Producer. If greater accuracy is desired, numerical readings can be taken. Research flatologist Dr. Michael Levitt was the first qualified person to insert a tube into

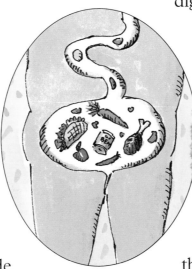

Left-over holding area

the rectum and measure chemical gases.

Q. *What is intestinal gas made of?*

A. Leftovers. As a partially digested dinner moves out of the stomach and through the small intestine, little finger-like projections called villi suck out the nutrients the body needs. What remains arrives at the portals of the ileocecal valve. This underappreciated one-way valve is a triumph of waste management. No matter what, it keeps waste from reversing direction. Once the waste is safely deposited in the large intestine, bacteria known as "intestinal flora" turn the undigested sugars into gas.

Q. *Why do people pass more wind as they get older?*

A. Dieting. Grains, green and leafy vegetables, fruits, beans, and Amstel Light are the staple ingredients of low-fat and high-fart diets. But probably the more common cause of excessive mid-life flatulence is a condition called "lactose intolerance" caused by an insufficient amount of the enzyme lactase, which breaks down the lactose in Nachos Fiestas and Chunky Monkey, making them easy to digest. As a result of this enzyme deficiency, the amount of undigested sugars in waste matter increases. It is estimated that up to one half of middle-aged people suffer from lactose intolerance, whether they know it or not. If they don't know it, someone should tell them.

Q. *What gives gas its distinctive odor?*

A. Methane makes the difference between low-octane aerophagic and premium high-test. Without methane, gas never can be important.

Q. *What determines what kind of noise gas makes?*

A. The laws of physics determine whether passed gas sounds like the squeal of a sneaker on a gym floor or the Fourth of July. As with a pinched or released balloon, the sound of flatus is related to the volume of gas, the distance of the gas from the sphincter, and the tension in the sphincter itself. For example, an SBD (the much admired Silent But Deadly) is colonically based, has traveled a short way, and met with little resistance. Given all the variables, the tonal and stylistic possibilities of gas are virtually infinite.

Q. *How much gas does the average middle-aged person expel each day?*

A. About 17.5 ounces (plus or minus 12)

Q. *How can my body tell the difference between gas and solid matter?*

A. The rectum can think. When the rectum dilates, it transmits to the brain the appropriate urge.

Q. *How long after a meal does the average middle-aged person start passing wind?*

A. Intestinal transit varies from two to six hours, which is why middle-aged people like to leave a dinner party by ten.

My Toys

My Personality

(Check where appropriate)

I am…

❑ A woman who loves too much.

❑ A man who loves women who love too much.

❑ A woman who loves men who are in touch with their feelings.

❑ A man who is in touch with his feelings.

❑ A woman who is sorry she ever said she loved men who were in touch with their feelings.

❑ A woman who runs with wolves.

❑ A wolf in sheep's clothing.

- ❑ A 50-year-old man who loves long walks on the beach and attractive young women.

- ❑ A 45-year-old woman who loves long walks on the beach and men who are grown-ups.

- ❑ A smoker.

- ❑ ....

My issues are…

- ❑ Rejection.

- ❑ Humiliation.

- ❑ Fear of abandonment.

- ❑ Other..

(Check where appropriate)

I am…

- ❏ In therapy.

- ❏ In a support group.

- ❏ On antidepressants. (I do ❏ do not ❏

    feel okay about taking them.)

I smile when…

- ❏ I get positive feedback.

- ❏ I get a tax refund.

- ❏ I have gas.

- ❏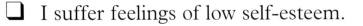

I cry when…

- ❏ I suffer feelings of low self-esteem.

- ❏ I see the "reach out and touch someone" TV commercials.

❑ I don't get my own way.

❑ ....

I get cranky when…

❑ My cocktail doesn't come fast enough.

❑ I have PMS.

❑ I need a change.

❑ ....

I laugh when…

❑ I'm feeling defensive.

❑ I watch Lucy reruns.

❑ I'm tickled.

❑ ....

Why...

Do gums recede?

Does it always rain on the weekends?

Do strangers half my age call me by my first name?

Didn't I make a list of my credit card numbers?

Why...

Do some people take up two parking spaces?

Are people my age running the world?

Can't I understand computer instructions when

they're supposed to be written for dummies?

Don't I get any real mail?

Why...

Do people collect collectibles?

Do fingernails get ridges?

Is it that the phone doesn't ring for days, and then all

of a sudden everybody calls at once?

Won't my children get married?

Why...

Am I always in line behind

someone with coupons?

Does time speed up?

Don't I feel any older?

Is the sky blue?

WHEN I GROW UP

It is never too soon to consider what kind of a place you would most like to live in when you grow up. There are a number of independent senior citizen lifestyle models from which you may choose. Some come with nutritionists. Some have country clubs. Some have special outfits.

One of the most popular plans involves selling the house and buying a condo somewhere warm where everyone is about your own age. You will learn how to pronounce angina. (The accent is on the first syllable.) You will complain that people are dropping all around you like flies. You will not drive at night. You will wear a pastel running suit and eat dinner at 4:30. The children and grandchildren will come to visit over Christmas vacation.

Another alternative, the extended care facility, promises to take care of you forever, no matter what, in exchange for all your assets, including the proceeds from the sale of your home. If you're healthy, you'll live in a town house, play golf or tennis, read great books in the library, fish in the freshly stocked trout stream, and eat meals prepared by a gourmet chef. If you get sick, you'll go to the facility's own luxury hospital. If you stay sick, you will go to their four-star nursing home. If you die, they get to keep your leftover money.

A third is the minimalist option: Don't sell the house. Tough it out alone. Get dinners from Meals on Wheels. Wear an electronic necklace connected to a central switchboard, and be picked up off your own floor by a total stranger.

In the last few years, communities of good friends have been discussing the feasibility of yet another alternative senior life-style, the Do-It-Yourself Retirement Colony. The concept is still very much in the talking stages: "We should all pitch in and buy an inn, or maybe a summer camp in upstate New York, or if that's too cold in the winter, maybe something somewhere farther south. Whatever, we've got to be on water, or at least near water. We'll live in the original cabins—we may have to winterize them—and eat in what used to be the camp's dining room. We should probably have microwaves or maybe even kitchens in each cabin, just to assure some privacy. But we could share the bathrooms. Or maybe we'd build extra bathrooms. Maybe even one for each person. With a lock.

"But the most important thing is we'll pledge to take care of one another—no matter what. If, God forbid, you are confined to a wheelchair, I will push you. We'll all push you. We'll take turns. You'll never have to be cared for by strangers, unless for some reason we all have to go somewhere together—we have theater tickets and the lift on the van is broken—and we can't take you."

Or, you can be a burden. All of the above model senior citizen life-styles are predicated on the counter-intuitive belief that children should not have to take care of their elderly parents, at least not in person. And parents believe—with a devotion bordering on fanaticism—that they must not, under any circumstances, be a burden to their children.

Why not? Why not be a burden to them? They were a burden to you. Didn't you love them, feed them, and sing to them when they couldn't sleep? Didn't you take care of them when they were sick? Didn't you change their diapers? Didn't you do your very best, never mind how they happened to have turned out? And you don't want to be a burden to them? What are you—crazy? If not now, when?

Of course they should lead their own lives, although there's nothing wrong with the life you gave them. Who's stopping them? That doesn't mean you can't live their own lives with them. You'll need your own suite.

At a time when the American family is breaking down, when the foster care system pays grandparents to take care of their grandchildren, you are offering your services free. You are the embodiment of family values. You are the extended family everybody's been whining about for the last two decades. Your children and your children's children need you. Why stubbornly insist upon maintaining your precious independence when someone else can do it for you? Does it really surprise you that life requires yet another sacrifice from you? Go ahead. Be a burden.

My Big Birthday Party

YOU'RE INVITED TO A BIG _____
(FILL IN NUMBER)

BIRTHDAY PARTY FOR: _____
(FILL IN NAME)

So please come prepared
To make a nice toast;
An embarrassing reminiscence
Is what people like most.

And how about a present
To tax the ingenious;
Please no books on aging
And nothing shaped like a penis.

RSVP   DRESS: LOOSE CLOTHING

On the Day of My Big Birthday...

The national headlines: ....

The local headlines: ....

Air quality index: ....

Biggest grossing movie: ....

The scandal: ....

Best-selling book: ....

Highest paid anchorperson: ....

Celebrity criminal: ....

Genetic breakthrough: ....

Biggest tax loophole: ....

Most popular cheese dip: ....

Price of a standard face lift: ....

Price of a Classic Coke: ....

Other: ....

MY HOROSCOPE

ARIES

THE RAM
MARCH 21 – APRIL 19

You are pure energy and always on the move. With your ruling planet in Mars and your third mortgage in the first house, you are unlikely to retire to the sunbelt and start sending your children boxed fruit anytime soon. Trekking in Nepal is a real possibility for next Spring. So are dental implants.

TAURUS

THE BULL
APRIL 20 – MAY 20

You are stubborn, conservative, deliberate and full of it—the last person in your crowd to give up cigarettes and the first to complain about secondary smoke. Still, you're generous to a fault and would give away your frequent flyer points if they let you. Stop buying series tickets. You hardly ever feel like going.

GEMINI

THE TWINS
MAY 21 – JUNE 21

You are dangerously overcommitted. No wonder you feel stressed out so much of the time. Stop worrying. Your memories of not having been abused as a child are reliable. Mercury is your ruling planet so it's a good idea to avoid fish and get most of your protein from poultry.

CANCER

THE CRAB
JUNE 22 – JULY 22

Like your crustacean namesake you are hard on the outside and tender and vulnerable on the inside, which makes you the center of attention at 12-Step meetings. You like getting into bed right after dinner, where no one can hurt you. A typical Cancer, you tend to under-utilize your living room.

LEO

THE LION
JULY 23 – AUGUST 22

At last you are beginning to mellow. Lower testosterone levels give your loved ones some badly needed relief. With your ruling planet the sun and your element fire, you should wear total block, even in Seattle. Precancerous growths can be removed by a dermatologist, but they leave funny-looking white marks.

VIRGO

THE VIRGIN
AUGUST 23 – SEPTEMBER 22

Years of therapy finally kick in. Your high standards still infuriate your friends, but now it's their problem. Yours is lower back pain. It's time to consider a cruise for your next vacation so you won't have to drive or carry luggage. Don't give up on your dream. If anyone can figure out how to fax a pizza, you can.

LIBRA

Feelings of anxiety should subside as soon as you make a final decision about a long-distance carrier. By the way, it's not your imagination. The doctor who performed your sigmoidoscopy *was* your paper boy. Pasta turns out to be an excellent source of complex carbohydrates.

SCORPIO

Your element is water, your planet is Pluto, and your reading glasses are in your jacket pocket. Relax! Dementia's not your thing. Kidney stones are. You will pass them. As long as the lines on your thighs and belly fade by morning, your jeans aren't too tight. It's your skin that's loose.

SAGITTARIUS

THE ARCHER
NOVEMBER 22 – DECEMBER 21

You are charming, optimistic, easy-going, and affectionate and have a great sense of humor now that your serotonin levels have been chemically elevated. You are inordinately curious about and proud of everything that comes out of your body. Don't be afraid to ask the waiter to repeat the specials.

CAPRICORN

THE GOAT
DECEMBER 22 – JANUARY 19

Stable, mature, and sane from birth, you were born for middle age. You have never had an inner child, a mid-life crisis, or a red car. You are the first in your age group to start commenting on how sloppily dressed and terribly rude young people have become. Winter is getting on your nerves.

AQUARIUS

THE WATER BEARER
JANUARY 20 – FEBRUARY 18

Your friends love you for your high spirits, uninhibited ways, and the witty messages you leave on their answering machines. Try to remember that your sign is water, not asphalt, so unless you're into knee surgery, stop jogging and start swimming laps.

PISCES

THE FISH
FEBRUARY 19 – MARCH 20

With water as your element and Neptune as your ruling planet, you are unpredictable, sensitive, and dreamy. A plastic flower on your car antenna could help. This is the year you begin to think of decaf cappuccino as dessert.

Living Will

of

_____

(PRINT FULL NAME)

_____

(HOME ADDRESS)

_____

(NAME OF LOCAL HOSPITAL)

If the time comes when I am incapacitated to the point that I can no longer actively take part in decisions for my own life and am unable to direct my physician as to my medical care, I wish this document to stand as a testament of my wishes should it be determined that I am in an irreversible, persistent vegetative state. Plant me.

_____   _____
                                                                     (DATE)

_____   _____
(SIGNATURE)   (DATE)

WITNESS: _____   _____
                                                                     (DATE)

WITNESS: _____